58 Missing Prophecies
Of Nostradamus

Amir.M

Translated by

Susan Sepehr

Copyright © 2012 Amir. M

ISBN: 978-1-939123145

Publisher: Supreme Century, USA

Prepared for Publishing: Asanashr (www.asanashr.com)

To Contact the Author: amirfictionnovel@gmail.com

Table of Content

1- Frightening Angel

All of a sudden a white, dazzling light covered everywhere, and spread in the air very fast. The radiance was so strong that you thought it may rooted in a nuclear bomb. At the same time the classical music filled the air and got louder and louder until the eyes of a muscular, thirty-year-old man who was lying down on a wooden bed started to open. The mattress was formed in the shape of his strong, muscular body that you would think he had been spending all his life sleeping. You could still hear the music. As the man was trying to open his eyes, with his left hand he grope toward the sound and succeeded to hold the small alarm clock, which was sitting on a small table, and turned it off. As he was opening his eyes and the dark surrounding got clearer to him, his face changed more, now there was no music and the silence which filled the room made him perplexed. Suddenly he came around and with stupefied eyes he stared at the bedroom. Even though he was still in bed and feeling the pressure and weight in his body, he tried to hinder the awful feeling which attacked him, as if he is hollow inside. How can a person identify himself when he cannot even remember his name?

Bewilderment surround you and you try to fight with all your strength to remember something form your past so you can hold on to. Just like a person who is falling form a cliff and tries to grab something for support even if it is a very feeble rock which cannot bear his weight. He was trying to find the answers for the questions which were plunging in his mind and made him more confused. There was an old round pine table in the middle of the room, a small shelf on the right wall with dusty books in it, a green Backpack with gray, black and brown colors which reminded you of soldiers in the war with a fishing rod sticking out of it were beside a closet beneath the window. These were the other possession you could see in the room but none of them looked familiar to the man. Uneasiness rolled in his eyes, but the only thing he could remember was that dazzling light and nothing more. What had happened to him?! Was he the only nuclear bomb survivor?!! He was static like a statue in the middle of his bed. Maybe he was surrendered by the questions which were turning and twisting in his mind and drawing his mind toward themselves.

No matter how hard he tried to find an answer for these questions, it was useless. It took him a long time to decide to come out of bed and look for a sign to get him out of that perplexity. He put his feet down which was as heavy as iron, but his black army boots did not let him to feel the hardness of the brown wooden floor. As he got up, the bed creaked loudly and he had to lean on to the side of the bed to control his balance so he could stand on his feet. He hadn't walked a few steps that the reflection of sun on a white piece of paper lying on the wooden table drew his attention. There was a white folded letter with a ticket next to it. With curiosity he picked up the white letter and he peered his eyes trying to read what was written on it. It was written: "Mr. George Jackson! I know that you do not remember anything and not know where you are, but you have to leave this place immediately because your life is in danger! The ticket on the table is a cruise ticket which leaves at 8:30 in the morning. Pick up the ticket and the green back pack which is by the wall quickly and leave the house as soon as possible. There is a red car waiting for you which you can see from your bedroom window which is not far from your front door.

Get into the car. The driver takes you to the port. When you get on the cruise, start fishing on the deck of the ship, so Mr. Michelle Faulkner can find you. He is a genetic professor and he will explain to you what had happened that you lost your memory. He informs you about the danger you are facing. Mr. Faulkner is about sixty five and well dressed. We shouldn't waste more time, Good luck."

Now the feeling of perplexity was mixed with fear and made his puzzled world vaster. At least, he knew, his name is George Jackson and it was the only thing that connected him to his past. The question who he has to find to ask and get more information had been something he, himself could not find an answer and now it was something he could hold on to and lean on. But he hesitated and his face froze. He thought how he can trust the letter when he does not even know who the writer is. How would he even know his real name is Georg Jackson? He thought to himself maybe he is an important person and some people want to take advantage of his amnesia. He was deep in his thoughts that something else came to his mind, what if his life was in danger? Suddenly he remembered 8:30 in the morning. What time is it anyway? What if the letter was real and it was past 8:30, then what he had to do?

Maybe he could never meet Mr. Faulkner. Then as he was holding the letter, he put the ticket in his shirt pocket and ran to the small table beside his bed quickly and he anxiously gazed at the clock. It was 7:16. He breathed with relief and relaxed. Now it seemed he had enough time to get to the ship, but another point was cleared to him. The alarm was set by the same person who wrote the letter and did not want him to over sleep. But who was he? Why

7

instead of setting the alarm he himself didn't wake him up. Finally he looked away from the clock on the table and walked toward the white framed window and looked through the hazy glass very carefully. He was looking out so suspiciously as he was looking for a murderer. He could see a red car parked across the street. It was far enough that he could only see a chiaroscuro of the driver's face. Maybe the driver and the person who wrote the letter are the same. It was another question that came to his mind. In order to find an answer he had to come out of the house. Maybe it would be better to search the house more before getting into that strangers' car. Time was vital for him, but maybe he could find some clues to give him enough courage to make a decision. Then he took a deep breath, as he was trying to stay calm and control his anxiety. He put the letter in his shirt pocket and began searching.

The deadly silence of the house was proof of him being alone in the house. But if there were another person in the house, it would be better he did not know about him being there. At first George walked toward the small bookshelf. Maybe the dusty look of the books brought back a strange feeling inside of him. It was a supernatural feeling. He wanted to go to different parts of the house and make sure he hadn't left any clues behind before leaving. Books were the first interesting object that attracted his attention. Between the dusty books on the shelf, there was a book with half torn cover which made it impossible to read the

8

name. But some energy inside attracted him to it. The feeling was so strange that made him pick up the book and turn the pages. The smell of old paper brought back a strange feeling inside him. As was turning the pages of the old book, his fingers stopped on page 217. Some words of this page became bigger under his eyes. He could not look away or see anything else, except those words. It was as there was a magnifier on his eyes to increase his precision to read those words. He started to murmur and read the words :

"And God gave his special angel his highest power and

taught him a lot. But a time arrived when the special

angel's disloyalty was revealed. Then at this time God

took back his beauty and turned him into an ugly,

igneous ogre. All his white feathers covering his wings

were burned, and his wings were turned into big, ugly

baths' wings. Then black, twisted horns started to grow

out of his head. The angel who now was turned into a

demon swore to take his revenge, so he flew away and

disappear from the sight"

When he finished reading the last word, suddenly a severe headache came over him. For a moment blurry pictures ran though his mind, like playing a film back and forth in front of his eyes so fast that he could not even recognize the colors. Unwillingly the book fell out of his hands while his eyes were shot closed due to the pain. He put his left hand on his forehead and pushed hard, maybe he could lessen the pain. But after a short period of time the pain was gone and a few seconds later, there was no sign of that awful pain. It was a mysterious headache that seemed not normal to him. He bended very slowly to pick up the book, right before his fingers could touch the book, suddenly he heard a horrible knock.

He turned his head toward the sound. The sound was coming from the narrow corridor which turned and twisted and led to the front door. He stood straight as he looked suspiciously around, walked slowly toward the sound. The sound repeated again, it sounded like someone hitting the door with a battering ram. It was clear, someone or some people wanted to force themselves into the house. As soon as George came out of the room and entered the hall, the white, wooden door broke into pieces in front of his eyes by the third kick. A person with boots black pants and bullet proof vest with the word 'police' on it came in. His face was covered with a black mask just like a SWAT team, and except his blue eyes the rest of his face was covered. For a minute with his determined eyes, he stared at George who was standing close to the bedroom door. Maybe he wanted to make sure he is the person he has the order to kill.

A big gun which he was holding very tight with his black gloves was pointed at George and a red; laser light coming out of the gun spotted his white shirt. The sound of bullets being fired were deafening, and with each shot, pieces of woods which were the result of destruction of hall's wall, were scattering in the air. It was like their slow motion was being played very slowly by a professional movie camera. George had had the chance to throw himself in the room. The sound of heavy boots hitting the wooden floor echoed and got louder and louder. A person who seemed to be part of the SWAT team was getting closer to the bedroom.

George jumped up and locked the door with the key that was on the door. Maybe it would have been better if he took the letter's warning more seriously and left the house. His heart was beating very fast and he was panting. The sound of steps being taken in the corridor reminded him of death getting closer, and it was hitting him like a sledge on the head. Now he knew, he had no choice but to do as the letter told him to do. He opened the window while he could hear bullets hitting the bedroom door. He looked at the street anxiously and then jumped out of the window, holding his backpack. Small bushes and grass which had grown under the window held him like a soft mattress. The bed room door broke down and the shadow of the deadly gun reflected on the wall. The gun was getting closer to the window by minutes.

He had his eyes focused on the car and running toward it with all the energy he had. His legs didn't feel heavy any more. He could only hear his own breathing mixed with his heartbeat. Exactly at this time, the laser gun came out of the window and that red light started to follow George. But before it could have a successful shot, George opened the car's door very fast while he was holding his backpack dived into the back seat.

It was then, that the driver who had headphones in his ears, turned his head and with surprised eyes as he was taking the head phones out of his ears, looked at him like his was some kind of alien falling from the sky into his car. Probably the headphones he was using to listen to music didn't let him hear the gun shots and was just lying on his seat relaxing. George who sprawled out on the back seat raised his head a little higher as he was trying to breathe and swallowing his saliva said, "Drive. Hurry "

The driver, puzzled by George's behavior, was still looking at him. Suddenly another bullet was fired and the car's back window broke into pieces. The gun shot, breaking the car's window and George's scream which said "hurry drive". All these made the driver realize what was happening. As he was holding his head with fear, he turned the key and the engine roared into the air. He pushed the gas pedal as hard as he could. Now the car was swerving from side to side and was getting further and further.

2- Mysterious Man

 Silence was filling the air in the car and nothing except the engine's noise, which changed when the gear was shifted, was heard. It's been two minutes since that awful, frightening event and George's attempt to get into the car. Now his body was deep into the leather back seat. He felt safe and relaxed. The ecstatic feeling you get when you are rescued from death. The same feeling when adrenalin is increased in your body. Even this feeling couldn't prevent him from asking questions that were in his mind and drove him crazy. He blamed the driver, who didn't rush to help him when his life was in danger, for the incident. Then without any instruction and before the driver could ask anything, he raised his voice and with angry tone said, "Who am I and why didn't you come inside the house to rescue me?" While I was fighting for my life, you were enjoying the music, and ……..

The driver while he was focusing on the other cars in front and passing them, looked at him from the corner of his eyes through rear mirror and interrupted his machine gun questions with objective tone said "look sir, I don't even know what you are talking about and I do not know you, yesterday a tall man who was covering his mouth and nose with a white mask gave me lots of money. He asked me to wait for a thirty year old man here at 7:30 in the morning and take him to the port. Of course, he told me to take care of myself and I should not leave without you under any circumstances. If I had known it would be like this, I wouldn't have accepted the money and come here. Now I will do my duty and take you to the dock, after this I hope I never see you again, because I'm not looking for trouble."

As he was trying to take over the front car, he shook his head and made facial expression to show his disagreement and groan with his mouth closed. You could hear the noise through his nostrils. Mr. Jackson, who didn't have any answers, went deep in to his thoughts and said nothing. Talking to the driver was useless. Now he wanted to meet Mr.Faulkner as soon as possible, so he could find answer for questions which drove him crazy. The red car was moving toward the port passing the cars on the way.

The sun ray was coming down through the tall trees on the way and reminded him of that white stunning light. George rolled down the window a bit, so he could feel the fresh air on his face and head. Maybe he was hoping the fresh air takes away all the disturbing thoughts form his mind .The wind didn't make a mess in his short black hair only he peered his eyes as the wind touched his face. It went on like this for a while, until the saltiness of the air told him they were getting close to the port. Anxiety filled his body. After ten minutes, George found himself in front of a number of ships, standing gracefully and lining up in the port. They amazed everyone

He had come out of the car a few minutes before without arguing with the driver or asking any more questions. Now he was searching for his ship between the others which were like floating cities in water. The sun was shining in the sky and everything looked calm. Finally, after walking for a while a ship with white, shiny body which was like an island coming of the sea, and its blue transparent glass that under the sun had an eye catching brightness appeared in front of him. The modern design and beauty of this five story cruise distinguished it from the other ships. Its name was written with big, blue color on its body was the same name he had on his ticket.

3- Fighting with the white shark

The ship slowly cut the heart of the sea and moved forward. George was sitting on a small chair close to the edge of the ship deck. He was holding a long fishing rod in his strong hands. Every now and then he looked around and he was still waiting for that 65 year old man. Suddenly his eyes froze on the railing of the deck, a few meters from him. A 27 year old girl's golden hair was dancing to the breeze and her long graceful legs were pushing her splendid body toward the railing, that only her right elbow on the steel railing was holding her and keeping her balance.

The way she stood her attractive curves, her sexy body, her shape and fit body, and the way she was leaning on the railing and the way her blue eyes staring into the horizon and not paying attention to anyone, all of these together reminded you of a beautiful modal from New York. But her black army boots, her green **bikini** which was exactly the same color of soldiers' clothes in the war was covering her body. The most important point which made her different form the other passengers on the ship were the two **katana** samurai sword which were strapped by two black leather belt on her back and formed the letter **X**.

George was experiencing a very strange feeling. He had not turned his eyes away from the girl that his fishing rod started to shake in his hands. He had no choice but to pull the fish out of the water, but every minute the fish got stronger. It was obvious, it was a big fish, and as it fought between life and death it used all its energy to free itself. Gradually drops of sweats were forming on his face and his hands were turning red. The struggle was going on, that suddenly the fish made a quick and fast move and George with his fishing rod were thrown in to the water. The sound of him hitting the water attracted people' attention on the deck and every one turned around. One of the passengers ran to the control cabin to ask the Capitan to stop the ship. There was a bigger event on the way. An enormous shadow with an unbelievable speed was emerging from the depth of the sea toward the surface and it was getting closer to George.

It was splashing and moving the water around it. George said to himself, "what's that?" Now he knew the struggle of the fish that pulled him into the water must have been to run away from this sea shadow. It wasn't long that a big fin came out of the ocean, and like sword cut the heart of the ocean, splashing the small drops of water leaving continues lines behind. That big shadow was a gigantic, white shark that was now after George because it had lost its prey. The shark's jaws were getting closer to him, that another shadow appeared but this one was not in the ocean. It was turning and twisting above his head and for a few second blocked the sun rays touching his face.

Sharks' jaws were very close to his arm, but before they could cut his arm, there was a very fast and powerful dive in the direction, where the shadow had been above his head. It was so fast and thunder like that you thought a sea bird had dived to catch a fish in the sea. The **katana** samurai swords danced in water and two deep cuts like cross were made on the left part of shark's fin. The white shark turned around in the water very fast. Now it was staring at the blond girl with its black frightening eyes. She was in water very close to him and was putting her wet swords in their sheath.

The shark that was provoked by the smell of its own blood turned and twisted in a mad way and attacked the girl. She was waiting for this attack. She put her legs together, curved her back, spread her arms on her sides just like the wings of a powerful eagle, then pulled them back toward her legs moved her body like a wave and started showing her **butterfly** swim. "What speed"!! She was swimming like a dolphin and with an unbelievable speed. Drops of water were splashing from the back of her black, heavy army boots, and at end of every twist and curve she gave her body with her legs she hit the water so hard that the water at the end of her ankle turned into powder and spread in the air, just like a racing boat moving with high speed.

She had started a mad race with the white shark. A swimming that loser will end up in the shark' mouth. The white shark was still chasing her everyone on the deck had rushed to the edge of the deck. They were watching this amazing race; they were so amazed that they totally forgot about George. One kilometer further a big cargo ship was getting ready to move, and it was pulling its enormous anchor out of water. The girl changed her direction toward the cargo ship and swam toward it as fast as she could. Nobody knew what she had in her mind and how long she can continue this anxious race. Both the girl and the white shark were getting close to the ship with very high speed. Now the shark's jaws were as close as two meters to the girl's ankle. As the anchor was being pulled out of the water, and lot of water was pushed aside. Now the anchor's big steel tips were about one meter to reach the surface. Before she hit the steel anchor for a minute, she reduced her speed and it was enough for the white shark to get close to her. Now the shark's jaws were as wide open as possible, but before the shark's teeth get the chance to touch the girl's body, in her last jump of butterfly swim she gave her back a big curve and with a fast and marvelous move, passed beneath the steel anchor and came out unharmed . But before the shark could have the chance to react, the sharp steel tips of the anchor entered its mouth and went through its palate. Blood spouted out in the air and no matter how hard it tried to free itself, it couldn't. It was hanging in the air and swinging from side to side. As the anchor went up, so did the shark's body.

4- Dark Wizard and the Secret of Beethoven Skull

Water was dripping on the deck. The girl with the blond hair was sitting on a small chair and she was running her fingers through her hair to take out the last drop of sea water. At this time, the wet black boots started to make noise on the shiny wooden floor of the deck, and his long shadow was stretching on the deck, and it was getting closer to the girl.

Yes it was Mr. Jackson who was coming close to the girl very politely, and he stood a few from her while the sea water was dripping from his clothes. He smiled and slowly looked at the girl's face and said, "Well, I wanted to say thank you. You put your life in danger to save mine. I owe you my life."

She smiled and playfully said, "Now, did you learn how to catch a fish?" I just wanted you to see, you can catch a fish without a hook and fishing rod. Did you ever think, you could catch a shark with an anchor of a ship?"

George smiled and said, "yes you are absolutely right, but swimming with that speed is like a miracle."

She said, "If you believe in yourself it is when the miracle happens."

George said, "exactly what steps you have to take and what you have to do to be able to swim with that speed?"

She said, "Only one step, you have to believe in yourself."

George that felt the girl is not interested in revealing her secret, and with those answers wanted to evade the question, did not ask anything else. Just to show he is a real gentleman he asked, "how can I repay your kindness?"

She put her pointing finger in her mouth and pressed it very gently with her white teeth, rolled her eyes up and as she looked pensively replied, "I'm really hungry. I swam a lot and I haven't eaten breakfast yet. You can invite me for breakfast in the ship's restaurant."

Mr. Jackson said, "of course, sure."

The girl said, "then we'd better change our wet clothes. I'll see you about fifteen minutes in the ship's restaurant."

Before the girl leaving the deck, George nervously said, "oh, by the way, I still don't know your name,"

The girl said, "I'm Elena, and you are?"

He paused for a minute and with a calm voice said, "I'm George."

The ship's hall was covered with a long red carpet, and the golden pattern of its wallpaper attracted attention. George now appeared wearing a black T-shirt which showed off his muscular body instead of that white long rolled up sleeves shirt, and his blue jeans and white sneakers which he took from his Backpack gave him a different look, but the new look did not seem important to him. Actually when Elena asked him, his name, she reminded him of something, the reason why he was on this cruise the first place. He had to find Mr. Faulkner very fast. Then, because of this before even going to his cabin and changing his clothes, he had asked the cruise staff to find Mr. Faulkner. At the end he had been so persistence that they even checked the passengers list, but it was clear that no one by that name had got on the ship. Now he didn't know anyone and no hope to know who he was. The only delight left for hi m was having breakfast with that beautiful girl who he had a strange feeling toward her. It was like she was part of him, was he really in love?

He didn't even know the reason to this question. What's more, he was facing another problem. When he was searching his backpack he realized he didn't have any money. His only possession was that Backpack, that's all. Now he couldn't even pay for one meal, but still the joy of meeting Elena who was waiting for him in the restaurant gave him a pleasant feeling. For a few minutes, he wanted to get away from thoughts occupying his mind, so he took a deep breath and walked all the way in the corridor which led to a big glass door with his white sneakers. Two crew members with black suit and bowtie pushed the glass door with their white gloves and politely said, "welcome", and he entered the restaurant.

A big rectangular room with glass walls, that you could see the ocean from every angle, and windows which were installed in the walls to suck in the ocean breeze. Many tables were set with exact distance from each other meticulously with the same white table cloths, vases filled with flowers, and classic music was playing. When the ceiling of the room moved away, you could see the sky while you were eating. All of these were the description of a luxurious restaurant on top level of a cruise ship.

Mr. Jackson glanced at the tables and then walked toward table 13. There were, two glasses of fresh orange juice a slice of Belgian cheddar cheese, two loves of fresh French bread that were still hot and their appetizing smell spread in the air. A few slices of ham which were cut very carefully, a small block of organic butter with golden color were all displayed on the table.

The newspaper was falling apart in Elena's excited hands, and she was following the lines with her shiny blue eyes.

She was so deep in readying that didn't notice Georges' presence, until he said, "sorry I'm late."

Elena pulled down the newspaper from her face and with an exciting face said, "George! You have no idea what had happened last night?" "The least noticeable one is a genetic professor being murdered." Then she pointed to the opposite chair and said, "Sit down, so I can tell you all about it."

As George was pulling the chair out very slowly, he noticed a young man's suspicious look at the table 10. He was lying back in his chair and every now and then he wrote something on a piece of paper. Elena slid the newspaper toward him on the tale and with an excitement that was covering her face, bended on the table and moved her finger in zigzag shape on the newspaper and said, "The strange news I was talking about it is here." As he was peering his eyes to see better, she started to explain with lots of excitement, "last night the skulls of **Beethoven**, **Nostradamus**, **Blackbeard**, **Merce Cunningham**, and **Michelangelo** were stolen in a very short time from each other. The interesting part is that witnesses had said a very tall old man with long white beard up to his chest with a black cloak and black cone shape hat had been the last person being seen before the skulls were stolen around the Nostradamus and Merce Cunningham's tomb. Of course some had seen a creature flying and carrying a big object

26

on its back in the sky in that area, but neither of them could be identified exactly what they were in the dark."

Then she rolled her eyes up, like she is a crime scene detective, she tried to look pensively and continued, "Of course, I think the theft of five skulls was done by the old man, but the question is how he can be in different places at the same time and so fast, and what he wanted to do with the stolen skulls. Another point is how, he could take the skulls out of the grave without making any noise to draw attention, and how he could steal the **Blackbeard** skull from the museum?" "any way, what do you think George?"

But she did not hear an answer. He was in another world. The time she was talking he was staring at the bold head line in the newspaper.

"Michelle Faulkner a genetic professor was killed in his house."

5-Gods' Treasure Map

Elena who did not hear an answer shook George's arm, so she could bring him out of the thoughts and dreams he was in. suddenly a severe burn mark with a pattern which was on his left arm, was exposed from his short sleeve. She asked, "What happened to your arm?"

At this time he came around and the first thing he said was, Mr. Faulkner.

She raised her eye brows and surprisingly said, "what do you mean? You mean Mr. Faulkner burned your arm?"

He said, "what are you talking about? What burn?"

She pulled his left sleeve up completely and said, "This burn"

Seeing the burn he felt strange and suddenly he had an awful headache, for a minute vague pictures passed his mind. He put his fingers on his temples, pressed and closed his eyes. Elena anxiously asked, "what's wrong?" "are you ok?"

A few minutes hadn't passed that his headache was gone. It was exactly the same as last time when he read the book. He took a deep breath and said, "no thanks" it's nothing"

She said, "if you my question upset you, I'm really sorry. I didn't mean to upset you."

George that felt at this situation, she is the only person he can trust and ask for help, took another deep breath and decided to tell her everything. He said, "That's not it. Honestly this morning when I opened my eyes …"

And he went on and told her everything that had happened to him with complete details. When he finished his story, immediately she started playing with her watch. As she was taking the watch close to her mouth said, "Hi, Charley get the helicopter ready. I'll send you the description of the cruise. Something came up that I have to come home right away." Please move as soon as possible. Thank you, bye."

Then with determined eyes looked at George and said," we have to get ready to leave."George who was really confused said, "I don't understand. Can you explain more?" She looked over very carefully. Then stared into his eyes and whispered, "based on what you had happened to you, it's not safe for you to stay on this ship anymore. Maybe those who wanted to kill you found out about you and Mr. Faulkner's meeting and some of them are on this ship. "From here we'll go to my house until we figure out what to do. Maybe you get your memory back and remember everything."

Even though he still couldn't believe she had believe everything he said, he hesitated for a few minutes and then nodded his head in agreement. But, why she believed him without any doubts and why she was willing to her life in danger to help him, was puzzling him. The restaurant was more crowded than before. They left the restaurant without even touching their juice. How can they be sure the breakfast hadn't been poisoned or someone didn't put poison in their orange juice? They went to the control cabin first, so Elena could talk to the Capitan about the helicopter which was going to land on the cruise platform. It was an around platform on the last level of cruise, in front of the main restaurant with a big black letter 'H'.

After she finished talking to the Capitan, they collected their stuff, picked up their backpack and went to Elena's room which was safer and waited for the helicopter.

George just hoped before something terrible happens, they can get on the helicopter safely to get away from all the negative thoughts. He wanted to entertain himself, so he turned on the t.v . A reporter as she was holding a yellow microphone ,was reporting " last night **Beethoven's piano** was stolen from the museum behind me, but the museum staff ….."

A few minutes passed like this until they could hear some noise outside in the sky. A red helicopter that the noise of its blades was like a huge insect flying in the sky appeared in the sky, and when they heard the sound, they went up the steal staircase to the platform. They got on the helicopter and sat on their seats. It shook as it was taking off. It got off the platform and headed toward Elena's house. A tall man through a white mask which was covering his mouth and nose with a heavy tone and very formal asked," Are you ok madam?" she said," I'm fine. Thank you, Charley. You are still sick, aren't you better?" He said," no madam, not completely. Elena said, "I hope you feel better soon."   He coughed twice and as he was trying to control the third one. said, "Thank you madam."

A very short conversation and then for a few minutes silence filled the air. George was looking outside through the arched window, that he was putting his head against it. It was like he was looking for something he had lost and maybe he could find it in the water beneath his feet or in the forest further that you could only see some green color, or in the sky above their head he was looking for his long lost memory. He really didn't know what to do, and how long he could stay in Elena's house.

If he could never get his memory back, then what?! Even though he felt safe at the moment, thinking about future frightened him. As he was deep in his thoughts he felt

Elena's warm hand on his shoulder. She put her head close to his ear and with her warm and sweet voice said, "don't worry. Everything will be all right." George nodded his head in agreement and smiled.

6-War plane pilot and the September eleven event

You could still hear the noise of the chopper's blades, when a big green land with very tall trees that you thought they were trying to touch the sky appeared in front of them. At the end of the land you could see a huge building which was more like a castle standing like a mountain tall with its long arched shaped widows around it. It was like a historical castle than a residential house.

Elena said, "finally we are here"

George staring at the building said, "is that your house?"
She said, "Well, of course it belongs to my ancestors, don't you like it?"

He said, "oh, yes, of course I like it. It is really beautiful"

As the chopper was getting closer to the ground the current caused by the blades made the green grass was covering the ground dance to the wind. The chopper landed with a little shake. Maybe now George could relax and breathe. They put their Backpack over their shoulders and walked toward the beautiful building, which was standing gracefully in front of them as they walked; with each step they took they could hear the green grass make noise beneath their feet.

They had walked about 100 meters that they found themselves in front of a big, wooden door with brass knockers which were really eye catching. It looked like a door of an ancient castle. It was like Elena, was taking George to see a museum. She opened the door, and they both entered the beautiful mansion. When the door opened to the beautiful mansion, it was a whole new world inside. The cool breeze running in the mansion gave you such soothing and nice feeling that you just wanted to sleep right there.

The entrance door was opening to a big Glorious, and mysterious room that you thought, the whole history must have had happened right there at once. The tall ceiling with classic drawing and unique plaster work was holding the drawings and its amazing beauty which was just like a church by Gothic architecturally captured human soul.

The luxurious chandeliers which were decorated with cut colored crystals, were hanging by golden chains from the ceiling. The floor was covered by black and white tiles and looked like a chess board. It was so shiny and clean, that you could see yourself in it. A white, marble pool in the center of the living room and a white marble angel which was cut to perfection and water was purring out of her mouth, in the center of the poor was attracting attention.

A big sky light which was installed in the ceiling reflected the light on the angel and it shone and gave it a special holly look. It was like a divine holly light shining on the angel from the sky.

Angel, Angel, this word repeated over and over in his mind. Yes, this angel and the light shining on it reminded George of that book. Again all the writings as big as before and as real as they could be, appeared in front of his eyes and the same strange feeling took over his body. He felt, he was drowning inside, and the same damn headache. The same vague pictures went through his eyes so fast; that he fell he was lost in a minute between the earth and the space. He put his fingers on his temples and pressed very hard. A few minutes later there was no sign of pain.

Elena asked looking worried, "again, you have headache?" With a warm voice he answered, "It's ok, it's gone."

Elena, "Do you remember anything?"

George, "No. like always the same damn vague pictures."

She pointed to the corner of the room, a few meters away and said, "You'd better sit down and relax." He didn't say anything and just followed her. Even though there was a few brown leather sofas arranged in a circle in the right corner of the room, she walked, straight toward the long, wooden dining room which was stretched up to half width of the room. It looked so old, that it reminded you the painting of Jesus last supper with his followers. There were 20 wooden chairs on both sides of the table in a neat line and the table even though it was very old, still looked great and standing still.

A man who was bold on top of his head, with an average height and polished shoes walked in and with a very formal tone said, "Hello, madam, welcome home." "I thought you would be away for the next four days."

Elena said, "Hello, peter. Something came up that I had to come back, by the way meet George" "As today he is living here and I want you to treat him the same way you treat me."

He didn't like what he heard and wasn't happy. To him George was an intruder. He didn't like to see his lady with any man. He believed no man deserved her. But it wasn't just that, he had a special feeling toward her, feeling that he didn't have the courage to say anything. As he was trying to hide his anger behind a very feigned smile, very polity said, "sure madam". She looked at George and said, "George, when I'm not around, if you need anything you can tell peter. He is the head of all the servants who work in this house."

Elena, "by the way, Peter tell the chef to prepare the food earlier today, let's say about an hour from now. George and I are very hungry, you can go now". He made a short bow and as he was clenching his fist, took very long steps and left. The sound of chairs being pulled on the chess tiles echoed in the room and Elena and George sat at the table. He looked at the expensive paintings on the walls and asked a question, which he should have asked much earlier than now, Maybe on the cruise or the helicopter.

He asked, "I want you to tell me about yourself". "Do you live here alone or not ...", and ..."

She smiled and said, "Well, we have about one hour until lunch is ready". She had a short pause and this is how she continued, "When I was 15 years old, I was accepted in a very well know company in New York as a model. I really didn't need the money but it gave me a great pleasure. I was studying and working as a model until one year later when, that accident happened on September eleven. It changed my life. My mother was in one of those airplanes that hit the twin towers. She with lots of other passengers was killed and this accident affected my life deeply. It changed my whole world. My goals changed and I felt I was another person.

I wanted to take revenge on behalf of my mother and all those innocent people who were killed in that accident, so I left modeling and focused on my lessons. A few years later I joined the American Army. I was the war plane pilot in the army. I participate in a few operations in Afghanistan, and bombed the area from air. I killed a few members of Taliban's group. At first I felt, I was on the right path and it was the goal, I was looking for, but in one of the operations the hiding place of Taliban was in a residential area and I bombed the place. After bombing I realized lots of innocent people were killed in that bomb attack. I felt guilty and my guilty conscience was driving me crazy.

I never wanted to kill an innocent person, well, I couldn't Continue. Every night I dreamed of women and children who were killed by me that's why I left the army.

My father who was an astronaut suggested I apply for space- shuttle pilot. It sounded good. Maybe this would help me forget that awful event. Time passed and finally I was accepted as a space – shuttle pilot. I participated in three space- shuttle missions but there was still that strange feeling inside me. An inner feeling, that was telling me I was created to do something bigger.

My soul was a challenging soul. Fight for justice. Fight for human freedom, but I didn't want to repeat that dreadful accident. So I decided to change my fighting method I told myself, after this I'll fight face to face, man to man. Maybe it sounds strange, but this feeling was burning inside me. Finally at the age of 25 I left the space- shuttle pilot and for 2 years I was trained by an old Japanese sword's man, who I could never understand why he had moved to America.

The night teacher gave me these two samurai **katana** swords which were his most valuable possessions before he died. I never leave them out of my sight, and carry them everywhere. About one month after his death my father died of cancer. I've been living alone for 2 months now. And…"

the time passed as she was telling him about her life. As they were still talking, peter arrived and with a cough tried to get their attention.

He said, "Excuse me madam, lunch is ready, can the servant set the table?"

Elena said, "Yes, of course."

She looked at George as she widen her eyes surprisingly said "how fast time flies."

Peter clapped his hands and the servants appeared. First they put a long, white table cloth on the brown, stratum table. Then two beautiful vases with white roses decorated the table. Silver, knives, forks and spoons were laid down.

After 5 minutes colorful dishes that were being put down on the table changed it to a beautiful painting. It was as the servants were creating a piece of art. After all the foods were laid on the table, peter pointed to the table and said, "What do you think madam?"

Elena smiled and replied, "It's perfect."

Peter held his head up proudly smiled and said, "You're welcome. Do you need anything else?"

She looked at the table and said, "No, thank you. It's perfect" Before leaving Elena and George alone to eat their lunch, he took his first step and stopped. He remembered something. "By the way madam, I forgot to tell you. This morning the phone in your room rang a few times. I think someone wanted to tell you something important, but because the door was locked I couldn't answer it."

She thought for a minute and then said, "thank you for telling me peter."

Peter, "you're welcome madam."

Then he had a short bow in front of her, coldly looked at George and as he was repeating something to himself left. As he was walking away, His steps echoed in the room and gradually disappeared.

7-Nostradamus Secret

There was still some vegetable left on Elena's plate and George was playing with the last pea on his plate with a fork, then Elena stretched her arm picked up bottle of Champaign from the table, looked at George and said, "Should I pour some for you?"

He took a deep breath and said, "No, thank you, I'm full, I have no room for food or drink."

She drank the rest of her Champaign and said, "I have to go up stairs. The phone call which was made to my office made me thinking." "You can come with me. So I can show you your room."

He nodded his head in agreement and said, "Hum! Ok."

They walked over shining tiles of the room and a few meters further, he saw himself in front of a long, wide and magnificent stairs which were covered with white marble and the railings of the same stone were holding them in their arm to the top.

When George was going up the stair, for a few minutes he had a special feeling, as the short, marble columns and stone railings were standing that way to show their respect to him. The way he went up was like Zeus was going up his palace's stairs.

But this unintentional feeling didn't last long and as soon as he reached the top of stairs, he felt like a normal person again. Elena's office was on the right side of the stairs. They went there first, a very beautiful room. The wall on the left was covered with big, wooden shelves from floor to the ceiling. Except a few picture frames, the shelves were filled with thick books on different subjects. Different honorary medals which were given to her in the army were attracting attention in the big, glass shelves on the wall on the right. The rest of empty space left on the walls you could see picture of space- shuttle and pictures she took of herself with her astronaut friends.

In short, it was a very crowded room.

Elena stretched her arm toward the yellow phone sitting on her desk and pressed the red bottom to listen to her messages.

"Hi, Elena, I tried to reach you, and talk to you, I wanted you to be the first person to know about this subject.

You don't know how excited I am. I really loved to see you and talk to you about it. But I have to get on a plane in a few hours and fly one thousand miles to attend a conference. The press is trying to get into the conference that I'm going to discuss this subject. There will be lots of bustle when I bring it up in the conference. Maybe lots of people disagree with what I say and they say I made all of it up. But I can prove all of it. Of course, I have a feeling, which tells me the Nostradamus skull being stolen has something to do with it and somehow has a connection. It's a very controversial subject. Well, I shouldn't waste your time any longer, and get to the point. Elena, to tell you the truth I made a great discovery. Do you remember the Nostradamus one hundred Quatrain prophecies? I mean chapter seven known as seven century?!!

The chapter that instead of 100 prophecies has only 42 prophecies and there is no sign or print of the last 58. Many people were thinking maybe the publisher for some reasons avoided publishing those prophecies. But I figured out what happened to those 58 prophecies. The night before the day they were going to print them someone got into the printing office and stole them. That person was no one except the Nostradamus himself. He stole his own prophecies, so they wouldn't be printed. I think now you are shocked after hearing this. Of course I'll be back in 3 days when I see you, we'll talk about it. Then we have to go after those last prophecies. I have really good clues that can help us in finding them. I just wanted you to be the first to know about it. Then prepare yourself for a real adventure until I come back. Bye for now."

Then Long beep was heard.

Elena was still staring at the phone. George came close and said, "Your archaeologist friend was very excited". "That's why you were looking at that newspaper with excitement."

The message was making George feel that she was hiding something from him. She sighed and said, "I'm not an archaeologist or historian, But Mrs. Hopkins is a history professor the one who left the message." Then she pointed to a silver frame which was in the middle shelf and decorated a picture of Elena. Putting her arms around a middle-aged woman and both were smiling. This picture brought back lots of memories for her. Memories of how close she was to her mother and remembering that took a big part of her heart to far, far away distance. The years she experienced the sweet, calm and safety of a child beside her mother was mixed with bitter feeling of losing her mother.

Her eyes were filled with regrets as she continued, "that woman is my mother." "After September eleven I attended the meetings which were held for the families of those who were killed in that accident. I met her in those meetings. She too, had lost a loved one, her daughter. Gradually we got very close, maybe you could say like a mother and daughter."

"In short, when one afternoon I went to her house for tea, she talked about a very important subject which was new to me. She said, the September eleven accident had been predicted by Nostradamus, and read some part of those predictions.

Some points were mentioned like, "Five and forty degrees, the sky shall burn" and "To the great new city shall the fire draw nigh." Then she talked about her decision.

She had decided to investigate all his predictions, hoping to know what will happen in future. Maybe this way she could save lots of innocent people's lives. She had made up her mind and she wanted to spend all her time on this."

"I accepted to help her whenever I had the chance."

George, who saw she was suffering, tried to change the subject and enthusiastically said, "Well, for now, we'd better forget about Nostradamus, whatever it is, Mrs. Hopkins will tell us all about it in the next 3 days. Who knows maybe three of us will go after the lost prophecies. It's a very adventurous and exiting work." "Isn't it right?" As she tried to bring herself out of past memories to reality, said

"You're right". "We have more important things to do now". George said, "more important things?!!"

Elena said, "Yes, important things." "Tonight we have to go to Professor Michelle Faulkner's house. Maybe we can find some important clues. But before we search for his house address, I'd better show you, your room and then everywhere in the house completely and you should know the rest of servants in the house."

The room was very nice. It had two big windows that opened to the green yard of the house.

There was a nice comfortable bed with white sheets, a desk and study light, two book cases filled with thick books, one long mirror on the right wall, a dresser with a nice mirror which had a carved wooden frame, and a wardrobe next to the dresser.

It was a woman's room and it had a special warmth and pleasant atmosphere. Elena said, "So, what do you think?" He glanced around the room and replied, "It's great".

Elena, "it was my mothers, she use it for her philosophic thoughts, and when she got tired, she lied on that bed in a meditative state, when she felt fresh again, she would sit at her desk and start to write. A few of these books on the shelf are written by her. She was a very unique person."

George, "your mother must have been a tasteful woman."

Elena, "yes, she was". "Well, now, that you liked gaur room. Let's go, so I can show you the rest of the house."

They walked in beautiful hall ways under plaster worked ceilings and passed walls which were decorated with beautiful and exquisite paintings. They went under arched shaped frames and went to the kitchen.

While she was introducing him to people who were wearing white cap and apron, they passed the crystalline glasses, pots, lades which were hanged like pendulum, vegetables which were cut into pieces in a flash by sharp blades, the heat of hot stoves and big cabinets.

They went around in the rooms of the house. Finally, when it was sunset, they relaxed on soft, comfortable mattress beside the covered swimming pool that was only a few steps below the house.

As George was drinking his orange juice with a straw, and preparing himself for the night of adventure, Elena was deep in her laptop, which was in her lap.

Everything was quiet until she shouted, "finally I found it". Then she turned her laptop and put the screen in his direction. He was walking toward her with the glass of orange juice in his hand and straw in his mouth, that Elena's eyes sparkled and said, "Luckily, his address isn't far from here". "It's about one hour by car." "Now finish your orange juice, we have to get ready for our adventure"

8-Search in the Dark House

Two flash lights, a magnifier, a few meter thick ropes and..., these were the stuff Elena was putting in her Backpack. Of course her old friends, the two samurai **katana** swords, were shinning on her back. She never went anywhere without them. Every minute there could be a man to man fight from unknown forces. Finally George and Elena entered a dark garage which was a few steps lower than the building and there was a steep surface with an angle of about 30 that lead to a green iron door.

She turned on the light and the light reflected on an orange **Ferrari** it was shining, just like a gem stone. A few million dollar car!!

George was really surprised and said, "This is fabulous!" she smiled and throw her back pack on the back seat.

When they got in the car that iron door went up. She took the steering wheel in her hand, pressed the gas pedal with her foot,the engine rumbled, the bright lights were shinning like panther's eyes in the dark.

The car jumped out of its place and went over the steep and flew in to the street. It was swerving as went toward its destination.

The car was heading toward Mr. Faulkner's house and the two bright head lights were glowing like panther's eyes.

The moon light brightened everywhere, but it wasn't as bright as the night before when it was full moon. After driving for a while, they entered the high way.

Elena loved diving fast, and the wide road gave her this chance to do what she enjoyed the most. Now, she could show her strength in driving too.

Exactly like drivers in formula one changed the shift gear and turned the steering wheel from side to side. She passed all the curves with maneuvering and high speed. As she passed another curve skillfully, proudly glimpsed at George who was sitting next to her and was stuck to his seat, he was so frightened that he pushed himself more into his seat. She asked with a naughty tone. "Are you enjoying the ride?" "If I knew the seatbelt wouldn't give you the security. I would have arranged a child's car seat in the back seat."

As his eyes were about to pop out, with faltering voice said, "me, me, I'm completely comfort table." "Actually, I love speed."

She smiled at him with naughtiness and turned the wheel very fast and passed another curve. It was a very quiet road and every now and then a yellow light from opposite cars passed their faces very fast. A few minutes passed like this, until finally she reduced her speed. They had passed all the twists in the road. Now, they were in a wide street and except the sound of their tires going on asphalt nothing else was heard. They were driving very slowly and Elena, with her sharp eyes looked carefully as she turned her head slowly.

Finally the car stopped.

As she was staring at a house with a gable roof, a few meters away said, very quietly, "number 63." she turned the key and turned off the car. She looked at him and said, "This is it." He looked around very carefully and slowly they got out of the car, they held their flash lights in their hands and went up the four steps outside of the front house.

They went under the wide, yellow ribbon border, in front of the house, which prevent them from entering the house.

They turned the steel door knob on the white, wooden door and the door creaked as it opened. She turned on her flash light and beamed the dark house with its circle light. The light beamed the face of a woman's portrait which was in a golden frame on the wall at the end of the hall way. There was a terrifying silence in the house. It was like entering a grave yard.

After George entered the house, Elena closed the door.

Their faces were in chiaroscuro and only with the weak reflection of their flash lights, their faces were recognizable.

Elena said very quietly, "we better divide the duties."

"We can get some results faster." "You search the rooms on the left and I search the rooms on the right". "If you found any clue or evidence let me know". He nodded his head and said, "Ok, good thinking, we do, as you said."

Professor Faulkner's house was more like a haunted house, and reminded you of horror movies. George didn't feel comfortable being there. The thoughts going to his mind made him anxious.

"What if some people with guns enter the house and the same event repeat itself? Just like what happened in his house!!"

"Can Elena's swords protect him from the bullets? His heart was beating so fast, just thinking about it. Anyway, very slowly He walked toward one of the rooms which were closer to him. He was trying not to think about that, maybe someone with a laser gun is waiting for him behind the wall. He went further. He could hear his own footsteps on the wooden floor. As he was swallowing his saliva and sweat was running down his face, he got to the door way and beamed the room with the flash light.

This time the circle light beamed a filling cabinet which was against the wall. He walked very slowly to the center of the room. He still didn't know what exactly he should look for. He decided to start his search from that cabinet. He held the handle in his hand and pulled it toward himself, suddenly he felt the weight of a hand on his left shoulder.

Really fast, he turned his head, as soon as he saw Elena's face, he sigh with relief, and took a deep breath.

She said, "Fast, come with me." "I found where they had killed professor Faulkner." They dashed toward the room which was on the other side of the hall. They entered Mr. Faulkner's office. Elena beamed the floor with her flash light, and said, "Do you see this big dark stain? It's dry blood". "I'm sure he was killed here."

Suddenly George noticed something and said, "Look over there!!" He turned his flash light toward something shinny. A steel object!!

The steel safe was crushed like a can on the wall. They went closer. When they looked at it more carefully, they noticed something strange. The steel door and body of the safe were crushed, but it didn't damage the wall a bit, not even a slight crack on the wall around it.

Elena said, "How, this is possible? None of the explosives or tools can crush the safe like this without damaging the wall."

George said, "Maybe, the person who killed Mr. Faulkner did this."

She said, "It's a big possibility." As she was holding the magnifier in one hand and the flashlight in the other, she tried to examine the safe more. But, to see the strange, black mark on the bottom of the safe, Flash light alone was enough, and she didn't need the magnifier. While she was showing George the sign, she asked, "Does this sign, remind you of something?"

He looked at it and said, "no, not at all, it doesn't ring any bells, it's not familiar"

She took a pen and a paper from Mr. Faulkner's desk top and told George, "could you please put the light on the bottom of the safe?" then she started drawing the sign on the white paper she put it in her Backpack.

She held her magnifier and flash light and as she was searching the floor said, "Could you search the shelves and the desk drawers, very carefully?"

He said, "Ok, sure".

Before he could get to the drawers of Mr. Faulkner's desk, the flash light he was holding in his hand, accidently beamed a calendar which was on his desk and drew his attention. Beneath one of the pages in the calendar which showed yesterday's date, something was shining, with lots of curiosity he turned a page and an address which had been written with a phosphoric, yellow marker appeared right in front of his eyes. There was a name of a woman beneath the address which had been written with a red marker. He tore the page out of the calendar and put it in his pocket. He didn't want to bother Elena, who was searching the floor at the moment. He walked toward the drawers of the desk and looked inside. He found papers, articles, a few fountain pens and lots of other stuff, but none of them was count as clue to George. He spent a period of time searching until a piece of blue paper drew his attention. It looked familiar somehow. He took the paper out of the pile of papers in the drawer. Although part of it was torn, he recognized it right away. It was a piece of the cruise ticket, which George had before, the time and the name of the cruise were the same as Georges.

George whispered, "Elena, look what I found."

She was looking at a big, Brown feather, she had picked up from the floor, she said, "What?!Did you find something?"

He got closer to her, as he was showing her the ticket said, "now, I have no doubt there is a connection between what Mr. Faulkner knew about me and his murder."

She said, "But, we still don't know what he knew about you."

George, "we'll find out soon enough". "Well", "what did you find?" She held the brown feather in his direction and said, "Only this. Of course it's big enough that I really didn't need the magnifier to find it."

He looked at the feather and said, "doesn't look, that, important" "probably Mr. Faulkner kept a bird in his house."

She put the feather in a plastic bag anyway, and as she was posing like a professional detective said, "Maybe things that don't look important, are important clues."

Suddenly a red light which was turning reflected on the wall dancing through the window on the south of the room. They heard a car stopped she said, "What the hell, the police is doing here." "Maybe one of the neighbors saw the light of our flash lights and called the police."

The word police to George associated with the same word which was written on SWAT team bullet proof jacket and the bitter memory in his mind. He got so anxious and nervous. He said, "Maybe they are the SWAT team, the same people who want to kill me."

Elena said, "We parked the car in the north side of the house. Which means we still have enough time to escape" "hurry up, we have to leave this place as soon as possible"

Very fast, he put his Backpack over his shoulder and both ran out of the room, and down the hall way. They went under the yellow ribbons and got into the car as fast as they could. Just as Elena turned the key and the engine rumbled, the police car appeared in Elena's side mirror from the back alley coming to the main street. Elena said, "Now I show them what driving is", "George! Put your seat belt on and sit tight, because I want to show you a real formula one."

She pulled the emergency break up, so the car would not move in front. Then she pressed the gas pedal as hard as she could, a very thick smoke came out of tires in the back. Now the orange sport car was like a bull making lots of dust by hilting its hoof on the ground and getting ready to attack. When the police car got within their five meters Elena pushed down the break and the car flew out of its place like a jet and went like a flash. After a few minutes of driving in a really high speed, Elena looked at her rear-view mirror; there was no sign of the police. She looked at

George sitting beside her and said, "It's weird! Why they didn't chase us?" George paused for a second, shrugged his shoulder and as his eyes were popping out said, "I really don't know!" Elena with her usual playfulness said, "Too bad, "you lost watching a great race." "Of course," "It was clear even before the race, that, I was the winner" then she winked at him with her right eye. But, why didn't the police chase them? It was a question, even, they, themselves didn't have any answer for it. They went through the same twisted road in the forest. The moon light was still everywhere and made the atmosphere more mysterious.

About one hour later the iron door made noise as it started to go up and the orange car entered the garage. Both of them were really tired and hungry. George was sitting in one of the leather chairs relaxing, as his arms and legs fell down from the sides of the chair.

Elena entered the living room with a tray in her hands from the kitchen. There were two ham sandwiches and two drinks on it.

She put the tray on the table which was in the center of the leather furniture and sat in a brown leather chair beside George.

George, "thank you."

She smiled and said, "After a real adventure and going to a haunted house, now it's time to build up our strength."

Then she picked up one of the ham sandwiches and took a big bite. George looked very tired. He said, "Damn the luck" "if the police hadn't arrived, we could probably find more evidence." Elena, chewing her sandwich said, "Don't be so sure, if you want to find any evidence, sings, or address the best place to look for them is the person's office, and we searched the place inch by inch. Didn't we?!"

George was staring at a place for a minute, it was like he remembered something, he repeated to himself. "Address, address" "the shiny address" "I totally forgot all about it." She said, "What are you talking about?"

He moved and turned his body to sides a little on the leather chair, so he could reach his pants pocket easier put his hand in his pocket and brought out a piece of paper.

He showed her the paper he had torn from the calendar and said, "This is the address I found on Mr. Faulkner's desk. Maybe it's an important clue."

She looked at the address and said, "Mrs. Smith". "This is great." "For sure we'll go to this address and ask Mrs. Smith some questions, but now, you'd better eat your sandwich and drink your drink, and don't think about anything, you must be tired. You have to rest tonight; tomorrow we have a busy day ahead of us."

9- Secret of Albert Einstein's Brain

It's 3:17 in the morning. The moon was glowing inside his room. He was lying on the bed and deep in sleep. It seemed nothing can wake him up. After all, he had an adventurous day. The whole mansion is dark and everyone except one person is asleep. Elena's office is not dark. Its light is on. But what is she doing so late?!!

She is working on something meticulously. Under her study light, she is concentrating on a card with white background and blue rim. On the left side of the card there is a logo, it's a circle with thirteen stars inside it.

Elena skillfully, is sticking her own picture on the right side of the card. In the middle of the card three blue letters are written **F.B.I**

It's 9:00 in the morning. The sun light has taken over the moon light. George is turning and tossing from side to side with his eyes closed. The white sheet is covering some part of his leg and the rest of it, is hanging by the bed and on the floor.

At the same time, someone is knocking at the door, and a voice said, "George, are you awake? I'll wait for you down stair, so we can have breakfast together." "OH, by the way, we have to go and see Mrs. Smith today.

You haven't forgotten, have you?" he was still half asleep and was trying to wake up, with a vague voice which was hard to hear said, ' ok. I'll come."

She didn't say anything else. You could hear her footsteps fade away as she got further. A few minutes later he was coming down the stairs, just like kings coming down. It wasn't his fault. It was like, it has been printed in his mind that he has to walk like this when he is going up and down the stairs.

His shoes hitting the chess tiles were like sledge hitting peter in the head. He was standing straight close to Elena and beside the dining table. When George got close, he said in a cold tone. "hello sir."

George. "Hello Elena, Hello peter."

Peter couldn't bear any man call his master by first name, so, as he was trying to hide his anger said, "I won't bother you madam, if you need anything call me madam."

Then as he was trying to avoid seeing George, kept his head up and went toward the kitchen.

George that couldn't understand why he acts like this said, "What's wrong with him? Does he have a problem with me?"

Elena shrugged her shoulders, as she didn't know and said, "That's peter. He has his own special personality". "By the way did you sleep well last night?"

He said, "I was so tired that I fell asleep before hitting the pillow, and didn't feel anything."

He ran his eyes over her and said, "You look different. Something has changed, this is the first time I see you without your bikini and in formal clothes, not any kind, a suit. Where are your swords?"

Elena, "today we have to go and visit Mrs. Smith, now you know why I'm dressed like this."

He smiled and didn't say anything. They had breakfast together, like always Elena drank her orange juice. About 9:40 again the orange car rumbled and they started their adventure.

This time they were going around in the poor section of the town, the part, where after dark nobody has the courage to walk alone. They still didn't know the relation between Mrs. Smith and Mr. Faulkner. Meeting her could answer this question. They were driving very slowly and they were staring outside through the windows, looking at houses very carefully.

Elena, looked at the paper from the calendar and then pressed the brake pedal with confident and said, "finally we are here."

Then she looked at George and said, "I want to ask you a favor, before we go down, please, Just let me talk first and from time to time just nod your head to confirm what I say, ok?!!"

Although George didn't know, what Elena had in mind, accepted and said, "Ok, agree."

He trusted her completely and this feeling was from the bottom of his heart. They got out of their expensive car.

Elena put her finger on the bell and pressed. A few minutes later a middle aged woman opened the old, faded colored door, but the chain that was closed behind the door, didn't let the door to open completely. From the small opening the woman looked at them suspiciously and said, "Can I help you?"

Elena said, "Mrs. Smith?!!"

The woman hesitated. "Who are you?"

Elena went a little closer and brought out a card out of her black jacket and very decisively said, "F.B.I", "We want to ask you some questions about Mr. Faulkner's murder." She looked at the card and said, "I told the police, whatever I knew yesterday."

Elena, "Mrs. Smith, we are working on this case specifically, so I ask you to work with us, please."

When Mrs. Smith saw how serious Elena was said, "Please, come in"

It was a very simple, but clean and tidy house. The furniture was neatly set.

Elena sat beside George on a very old sofa, crossed her legs and said, "Mrs. Smith, how much did you know Mr. Faulkner?"

Mrs. Smith was sitting in front of them.

She said, "Well, these ten years that I have worked for Mr. Faulkner, I can say I got to know him pretty well.

Of course, I should tell you, I know who killed him and probably you want to know the same thing, isn't that true?" George and Elena were shocked by what they heard. She continued, "Mr. Faulkner's murderer is that weird old man. He had an appointment with Mr. Faulkner at 8:00 in the evening. When he came at 8:00, they went to his office and were talking for a period of time. I don't know exactly what they were talking about. After half an hour, exactly when I was setting the table for dinner, that weird old man left the house in a hurry. But there was no sign of Mr. Faulkner. When I went to his office, I found his body on the floor and a knife in his chest up to the handle. It was a terrible scene." Her tears rolled down.

George got up and gave her a tissue to dry her tears.

Elena asked, "You had never seen that old man, before that night?" As she was cleaning her tears, with a shaky voice said, "No, never" I had never seen him.

Elena, "why you say, the old man was weird and strange?"

Mrs. Smith, "big , long, white beard, the black cape he was wearing , the cone shape hat that he had on his head and the big eagle with brown wings and white head that was sitting on his shoulder, everything, everything about him, was strange to me."

Elena, "the period of time that the old man and Mr. Faulkner were talking in the room, didn't you hear any loud sound, like an explosion?"

Mrs. Smith, "no, I didn't hear anything."

Elena, "when you entered the room, was the safe door open?"

Mrs. Smith, "I was shocked, when I saw the body, but the crushed safe door attracted my attention."

Elena, "then, the safe door, was open?!!"

Mrs. Smith, "yes, it was completely open."

Elena, "what did Mr. Faulkner keep in his safe?"

Mrs. Smith, "well, he kept his most valuable things and possessions."

Elena, "Mrs. Smith, can you be more specific."

Mrs. Smith, "As you know, after Albert Einstein death, Thomas Stoltz Harvey, doctor in Princeton hospital, divided Albert Einstein's brain into hundreds of microscopic slides to be studied more. Well, Mr. Faulkner had the chance to get one of these valuable specimens after a few years, so he could study on it. In fact, the specimen he had was a unique one and he kept it in the safe. The one that is crushed now."

Elena, "only one more question."

Then she put her hand in her jacket's pocket and brought out the paper , she had drew that strange sign, and as she was holding it in front of her said, "is this sign look familiar to you?"

She peered her eyes to see better and stared at it for a few second and said, "No, it doesn't look familiar, this is the first time, that I see this"

Elena said, "thank you, for your cooperation, I don't have any more questions."

Before she could get up George said, "There are still a few questions." "Was Mr. Faulkner supposed to go on a trip?" "For example a cruise?"

Mrs. Smith, "No, he wasn't supposed to go anywhere. Whenever he was planning to go somewhere, he would tell me a week earlier."

George, "we found your address in his calendar on his desk. If you have been working in his house for 10 years, why he needed to write your address in his calendar?"

Mrs. Smith, "he didn't write it. It was me who wrote my address on a page in his calendar. I moved here about 5 days ago and he asked me to write my new address for him. That's it."

George, "How did you know, what he kept in his safe?"

Mrs. Smith, "Mr. Faulkner didn't have any children or a wife. Since he trusted me completely, sometimes he would open up to me and tell me his secrets. Of course, I am a very trustworthy person, and if it wasn't about his murder investigation, I would never tell you anything, sir."

It was obvious Mrs. Smith was offended by his question.

He asked his last question anyway, "Are there any more secrets about Mr. Faulkner, which you haven't told us?"

Mrs. Smith answered coldly, "No. sir." "I told you whatever I knew."

He took a deep breath and said, "Well, thank you for your cooperation."

Then they both got up and went toward the door, they had come in a few minutes before.

They hadn't gotten into the car. That George said, "Wait a second," "are you F.B.I agent too?"

Elena, "George," "it was fake."

George, "what if she found out?!!"

Elena, "Even you didn't notice it was fake. What's more, I know my job very well."

George that felt it was useless arguing with her, he preferred to just get in the car.

The car rumbled and they headed toward home.

While she was changing the stick shift, asked, "Do you think she was lying?"

George, "No, I think everything she said, was true. You could see it in her eyes."

Elena, "I feel she was honest in answering the questions."

"But who is this weird old man who leaves a trace after himself in all these events." "How he could be in all these events in one night, so fast?"

George said, "I don't know. Maybe he flew like a jet ..." George hadn't completed his sentence that suddenly Elena pressed the brake pedal so hard, that if George hadn't put on His seat belt, he would have been thrown out of the wind shield. There was a squeal sound of tires in the street.

George, "what are you doing?"

People behind them put their hands on their car's horn and made so much noise. They shook their hands in anger. Elena didn't even pay attention to angry people.

Before George could say a word, she turned the steering wheel, pressed the gas pedal and turned the car around.

She said, "Why I didn't think of it myself."

There was a heavy smoke coming out of the back tires.

Now the car was going in the opposite direction of before in the street.

George, "could you tell me what is happening?" As she was taking over the front car said, "Do you remember the newspaper on the cruise?"

He looked at her surprisingly and said, "What do you mean?"

Elena, "the night that all those events happened, witnesses said, they had seen a creature flying in the sky and it was carrying a big object on its back."

George, "wait a minute! You mean the old man had used this flying creature?"

Elena, "yes, this is exactly what I mean."

George, "now, where are you going in such a hurry?"
Elena, "there is an air –force head quarter around here.
maybe they can identify and tell us what kind of creature it
is and where it came from and where it went, based on
what their radar had been recorded."

10-Flying Creature

The orange car passed a number of cars and gradually a long concrete wall which was hundred meters long appeared on their right side. The barbed wires on top of concrete wall showed how secure it was. The sport car took a detour that lead to air-force head quarter and stopped in front of the security check. Elena brought another card out of her jacket and showed it to a strong built man who was wearing army clothes. He looked at the card, and then he looked at Elena's face he nodded his head in improvement and shouted, "they can pass." The metal gate which was hanging about one meter from the ground started to go up in an angel and opened the way for them. The car took the asphalt road to the huge, tall building which was about 12 to 13 stories. On top of the building a big radar was turning around itself and a little further lots of big dishes on huge, tall, metal base that were touching the sky and big storages that were probably used for air-force planes showed up. They went up the stairs and again she showed her card to the two security guards who were guarding the entrance door of the building with guns and finally they entered the concrete building. She pushed a bottom that was on the wall beside a shiny steel door, and the elevator door opened. They entered and then she pressed the bottom which number 10 was printed on it. The door closed very slowly and very fast they went up, it hadn't taken 30 second that a beep was heard and the door opened to a long hall.

There were a number of rooms on both sides of the hall. Elena raised her left eyebrow and said to herself, "If I'm not mistaken, it was room seven."

They walked under the lights that made their shadow short and long in the hall as they were walking, they looked at the numbers on the doors and read them, 1, 2, 3 ....Finally they stopped on the door with number seven. Elena knocked on the door and turned the steel knob. When the door opened, the two men who were sitting behind the computer system turned their head from the black screen that a green light was turning in a circle on it and looked toward the door. One of them who had brown hair and was wearing very thick glasses got up with a smile. It was like seeing an old friend he went toward Elena and George. Elena ran toward him and said. "Arthur!!"

They hugged each other for a few minutes.

Elena, "you don't know how happy I am to see you."

Arthur, "me too, I haven't heard from you for ages", "by the way, who's this good looking man?!"

Elena, "oh, sorry, I forgot to introduce you two."

She pointed to Arthur and said, "This is Arthur my old friend and colleague. I have learned a lot from him."

Then she pointed to George and said, "This is my friend George." They shook each other's hands warmly and smiled with respect to each other.

Elena continued, "Arthur I wanted to ask you something, can you do me a favor?"

Arthur, "what can I do for you?"

Elena, "I wanted to know, about two nights ago around 8 or 9, maybe earlier or later, didn't you see anything strange on your radar or something weird in the sky in this area?" Arthur paused for a minute and then continued. "Of course, whatever we say should stay between us only. Actually 2 nights ago, we noticed a suspicious flying object that was flying in the 70° angel. We even sent two of our war aircrafts to investigate more, but the pilots didn't find anything.

It was like the object had disappeared and a few minutes later it was even gone from our radars. We were really confused, that's why we sent all the information which was recorded about this object, and its flying angel, to the space research department, and they took a few pictures of its flying direction in the sky."

"A few pictures were even taken by space telescopes, but unfortunately we haven't had any result and the identity of this flying object is still a mystery. By the way, how did you find out about this? Because of security reasons we haven't told anyone yet."

Elena, "it's a long story; I'll tell you all about it later in details. Just, can I ask you, E-mail me the pictures space research department sent you, please. Maybe I can help you in solving this puzzle!!"

Arthur, "no, problem, just please give me your e-mail address, I'll send you all of them."

Elena, "Do you have a pen and paper?"

Arthur, "I'll bring it now."

11-Human Clone

After they thanked Arthur, they said goodbye and got in their Iron horse, the engine roared again. It seemed their today's adventure was finished, but still there were new events on the way. When they got home, they were still going up the stairs from the garage that peter came to welcome them And said, "You have a guest Madam." "Mr. Hopkins is here. He doesn't look ok. When I told him you weren't home, he preferred to wait for you madam! I think he has something important to tell you. I asked him to wait in the living room, but he hasn't sat even a minute since he arrived and he is pacing the room, madam."

Maybe what made peter talk too much was Mr. Hopkins's uneasiness.

Elena, "Thank you peter."

Peter bowed and left. As Elena was walking toward the living room told George, "Mr. Hopkins is Mrs. Hopkins only son." "You know Mrs. Hopkins?!!" "The history professor?!!" George "yeah, I remember." "But what his son is doing here?" Elena, "we'll find out soon." His shadow was moving on the wall like a clock pendulum, he was so nervous. It was clear something had made his mind uneasy. But what was it?

They were still a few meters away from Mr. Hopkins, that Elena said, "Hello, Thomas." "I'm so happy to see you." Mr. Hopkins stopped in his place when he heard Elena's voice and looked at Elena and George. In his face you could see sadness, anger and confusion. He said in a rush, "Hello Elena, your number, was the last number my mother had called; I want to know what she told you?" The way he talked was more like an interrogator than a guest, or better say a criminal sector interrogator. Elena who was surprised by his sadness and nervousness her face changed and said, "What's wrong?!" this question was like cold water over Thomas. It was like someone froze his soul. He couldn't stand on his feet; he just collapsed in one of the leather chairs. As he was trying to take a deep breath to control his feeling and tears from falling, squeezed his lips, sighed and he was silent for a few minutes. Then he explained the bitter event that was hunting him so much.

"Yesterday afternoon, when I went home I saw my parent's body on the floor with a sword through their hearts. It was a terrible scene.

I had an awful night at the hotel. But this morning I thought of something. I went back to the house and checked all the phone calls. I noticed, the last call my mother had made to, was here. Elena you are the only

73

person who can help me," And a drop of tear rolled down his face.

Elena was shocked by the news and then with amazement said, "I can't believe it."

Thomas, "Elena! What did my mother tell you? The last time she called?" "This is very important to me."

In his sad eyes, there was some persuasion to know the truth.

As she had to fight back tears said, "When your mother called me, I wasn't home and she left a message. We can go upstairs, so you can listen to it." Thomas said anxiously. "No, not now, I'm not ready. Listening to my mother's voice when she's gone is very upsetting to me." "Can you just tell me what her message was about?" Elena, "she said, she had discovered something new about Nostradamus, and…"

She wasn't finished that Thomas interrupted her and said, "no, I didn't mean all these, I just want to know if my mother said anything about the organization?!!" "Of course, it's been quite a while, but it is possible my parents were killed by that damn organization."

Elena tried to fight back her tears, the harder she tried, the less she succeeded and her tears washed her face. As tears rolled down, she remembered the time she lost her mother.

She didn't want to cry like those days. She knew crying is useless. She tried to fight her tears back and thought of something else instead. Yes, she was thinking of revenge. As she was trying to control her feelings with all her energy said, "what organization are you talking about?"

"What subject are you talking about?"

Before Thomas could answer, George tried to make the atmosphere a little calmer, by giving each a tissue to dry their tears and asked them to stop questioning and answering even if it is only a few seconds. George asked a servant to bring two glasses of cold water for them. Thomas drank a little and put his head back on the leather chair. For a few minutes thought about his past and reviewed his memories. He sighed again and this time calmer wanted to answer the question Elena had asked before. He said, "Well, it's obvious, mother didn't tell you about this subject. It happened 27 years ago when I was only 5 years old. As you know my father was a genetic scientist. He was helping a research organization on cloning animals. When the organization was very successful in animal cloning, a few members of the company decided to use this ability for human cloning too. It wasn't long that a group of politicians, religion leaders' especially pop and even well-known people showed their disagreement against this subject. All the organizations that were working on cloning were not allowed to work on human cloning legally. But 27 years ago something strange happened. One night my father woke up frightened. He dreamed of a young man with white wings full of white feathers coming out of his shoulders came to earth from the sky. The young man had a clean, long white gown on and he had a beautiful face. This is how he introduced himself to my father, "I am God's special angle and I have a command from my God to you." Then he showed my father a few small bottles and this is how he continued "You have to clone a human with what is in these small bottles, a human who is different from all humans, a fighter who fights for God only. There is a big war in a faraway place. Whatever I told you is God's command."

Then he spread his white wings and flew a way to the skies. The next morning, when my father went to work, he saw exactly the same small bottles on his desk. He had no doubt that it was a mission from God and he had to obey. He had been working on this project secretly until he succeeded in cloning human. My father brought the cloned baby home, but two weeks later, in a cold and bright night when the moon light was covering the earth, something really strange happened. My mother had gone to the kitchen to bring a bottle of milk for the baby. When she went to the room, before she could even turn on the light, she saw a man under the moon light in the room. The old man had long, white beard, black cloak and a long cone shape hat. He was standing in the middle of the room, holding the baby. My mother screamed as she was so frightened and the old man while he was holding the baby broke the window and jumped out, he disappeared after a few seconds. If anyone would find out about my father had cloned a human, the whole organization would be in trouble and millions of dollars of budget would be cut forever. Of course, after a while, the organization offered my father secretly to work on a project for army, but he didn't accept it, and three months later he resigned and left the organization. We've never known what the project they wanted my father to work on, for the army, but I have a feeling the organization killed my parents."

While Thomas was talking, George put his fingers on his temples and pressed for a few minutes, but he tried that nobody would understand he had headache. Some parts of his conversation had made those vague pictures fill his mind again and made him have an awful headache for a period of time. Thomas was still talking that his cell rang. He apologized for a minute. When his conversation had finished his face was changed.

Thomas said, "It was the police, they wanted me to go there apparently they have new information." He got up.

Elena, "Let me know, if you found something."

Thomas, "sure."

He hugged her and shook George's hand and left the house to go to the police station.

12-The 58Missing Prophecies of Nostradamus.

Elena was nervous. Now that Thomas was gone. Elena was pacing the living room in his place. Suddenly she stopped and with a look full of anger and sadness said, "This damn puzzle must be solved. I have to know, how these events are connected to each other! I'll find this murderer."

She didn't say a word after that and seriously went toward the stairs. George, "where are you going?"

As she was still continuing her walk said. "I have to listen to Mrs. Hopkins's message one more time. Maybe I can find some clues."

George got up, as he was following her said, "Maybe, it's better together, we listen to it again."

The sound of their feet echoed in the room. Elena was putting her hand under her chin and a look which was more like a criminal detective, reviewing the crime scene in her mind, was staring at the phone. Again the long beep on the phone showed the end of the message. She looked at George and said, "Did you notice anything?"

George who was standing in the middle of room with his hands folded sighed and said, "this is the fifth time that we are listening to this message! If there were any clues regarding Mrs. Hopkins death we would have noticed, don't you think so?"

Elena, who was sitting on her desk, jumped down and started walking around the room, trying to collect all her knowledge at once and said, "Let's review all the events again. Mr. and Mrs. Hopkins and Mr. Faulkner all three were killed the same way. Mrs. Smith is saying the old man in black killed Mr. Faulkner. If we think all three were killed by one person. Then Mr. and Mrs. Hopkins' murderer must be that old man in black."

George,"but something here is not right!" Mr. Faulkner knew me; we were supposed to meet on the cruise. Then, if they were planning to kill me after Mr. Faulkner, that morning, they should have sent that weird old man to the house, not the SWAT team."

Elena, "by the way, do you remember that address? Maybe we can find new clues?"

George, "at that moment, all I could think about was to stay alive. I don't even remember how I escaped from there; let alone the address of the house!"

Elena, "then we have to solve the puzzle with whatever we have now."

George. "Maybe, Thomas was right!"

Elena, "what do you mean?"

George who was trying to speak more rationally said, "Both Mr. Faulkner and Mr. Hopkins were working in genetic filed. Maybe they were working on a secret project or maybe they just wanted to stop a secret project and reveal some information. That's why they were murdered by the organization." Elena as she was opening the window said, "but, I think this theory can't be right. An organization as modern and high tech as this with budgets of hundreds of millions of dollars, if it wanted to kill two famous genetic scientists, would kill them without any one notice like a fake accident, using poison or at last it would hire a professional hit man to shoot them. It would never hire a swordsman."

George, "I think, you've right."

Both were deep in their thoughts for a few minutes until George broke the silence with a different question this time. He said. "maybe, Mr. Faulkner didn't know me at all, Mrs. Smith who worked there for ten years, when she saw me, it was like she is meeting a stranger. It means these ten years I hadn't been there even once! If we weren't very close to have relationship or see each other a few times, why would he risk his life to meet me? Perhaps, we weren't supposed to meet on the cruise at all! Mrs. Smith mentioned that Mr. Faulkner wasn't supposed to go on any trips, or maybe he was planning to go home by his private helicopter after getting on the cruise just like us, which I doubt it. I don't think he had a private helicopter."

Elena, with eyes popping out , shook her head in protest and every time she shook her head said, "maybe , but, if" then she put her hands on the window frame and took a deep breath from the air out side. She filled her lungs with fresh air to feel calmer.

George was still standing quietly in the middle of the room. Elena turned her head and looked at George and said, "Excuse me!! But George! These words wouldn't solve any problem. Didn't you find that cruise ticket in Mr. Faulkner's desk!" "Didn't you say; now you are sure, since you found the ticket?!" "See George! This puzzle might be more complicated than we think." "We don't have all the information about this puzzle to solve it, that's why the more we think, the more we have confusion and contradiction. But we can solve it another way, or better say instead of solving it ourselves we can use the person, who can give us enough information and all these events lead to him."

George, "what do you mean? I don't understand?"

Elena. "When you want to solve a puzzle you have to look at it from top. You don't need to know all the details. If you look at all the events that have happened these past few days, what do you see?" "Mrs. Hopkins is murdered when she found a big secret about Nostradamus!!" "We also know skulls of Nostradamus, Merce Cunningham, Blackbeard, Beethoven and Michelangelo were stolen the same night, and who the witnesses see before the skulls were stolen around the grave yard?" "Who stole that cloned baby from Mr. and Mrs. Hopkins house?" "Who kills Mr. Faulkner?" "In all these events you see the trace of that old man in black. Maybe we don't know all the details, but what we know is that all of them lead to him. Then we have to focus on, only one thing. We have to find that old man in black!"

Elena's words had convinced George, but still he asked another question. "Where should we look for him?"

Suddenly she got up walked toward her laptop which was on the left side of her desk and said, "Good thing you said it. I completely forgot all about Arthur. By now, he must have sent the pictures, for now these pictures are our only hope to find the old man."

 The lap top has been on for one hour now and both of them were looking at the screen very carefully.

At last George moved his neck and as he was trying to control his yawn said, "All of these pictures are the same I don't see any clues in these thirteen pictures. I think …."

Suddenly he stopped completing his sentence. Elena, "what happened? You were saying?!"

He moved his head closer to her and quietly said. "Look at the window's edge."

What had surprised George was an eagle with white head and brown wings looking carefully around the room with its sharp eyes, and was holding to the window's frame with its powerful claws. Elena got up very slowly and walked toward the eagle and when she got close enough, very slowly took the rolled papers from its yellow beak. Now she was holding 2 pieces of old papers, but the quality of 2 papers were different. The eagle that had completed its mission successfully, turned his back at them, spread its big wings and flew away. After a few minutes it was like a spot in the heart of the sky. As Elena was opening the old papers curiously, very slowly and carefully, George got close to her. But he wasn't able to read what was written on the first page. They were mixture of different languages like, Greek, Italian and Latin. The smell of old paper filled the air in the room and Elena like an archaeologist in an amazing way was translating the words in her mind and murmuring :

"Seven century, 43, that night will arrive. The night that an army of prophets in white in front of an army of wizards in black will line up like chess-men in chess. A battle that you have been waiting for thousands of years will start, but another battle is on the way."

There was a strange symbol at the end of the quatrain. It was exactly, like the black symbol that was on the bottom of Mr. Faulkner's safe.

After Elena finished reading this, she started thinking for a moment.

As George was looking at her said, "what language are these writings in?"

Elena was staring at the paper, as she was remembering something said. "Nostradamus."

George said surprisingly, "Nostradamus?!!" "What do you mean?"

Suddenly she screamed excitedly like she discovered something "Nostradamus! Oh, my God!! These are Nostradamus' missing prophecies!"

George, "How can you be so sure?"

As her eyes were still sparkling with happiness and her voice was trembling with excitement said, "I have seen his hand writing before! Mrs. Hopkins showed me some writings, which were written by him a few months ago. Then without giving him time to ask another question enthusiastically continued reading the prophecies: " **"44"**, the final battle will happen in front of Gods' gate, anchors in fire will turn in the sky to destroy the columns of the gate". "There will be a hard battle in the sky and in the sea. The big tower will fly in the sky,

" **45"** fairies of the sea will sing." Fairies of the swamp will dance. The black and the white power will mix together. Angels of death will stop going,

" **46"** the old man in black will pull the bones out of earth. He will disappear between the stars; he will enter the dark hole, the place where the biggest battle of

universe will happen."

Elena and George were frozen by the forty sixth prophecies. The two clues were in the prophecy. First of all, at end of each quatrain the same strange symbol they had seen at Mr.Faulkner's house was printed. And second, it was explaining exactly what had happened 2 nights ago. Elena was so excited to read the second paper and the rest of the prophecies, but the second paper wasn't the same as the first one. What shocked them wasn't the quality which was different from the first one but it was something else the difference was in the sentences which were written on the paper. Even George was able to read them. Then they read the written words." do you want to read the'47' and the rest of the prophecies." "Then you have to look for me, because I'm the only one who has the missing prophecies, but I don't think you have enough time, because you are weak creatures and your planet will be destroyed very soon. Then, instead of looking for me you'd better prepare yourselves for death."

Still, a few seconds hadn't passed from reading those sentences that Elena bite her lower lip with anger and as she was crumpling the paper in her hand, with a voice full of anger said, "I will find this damn old man wherever he is" then she threw the crumpled paper in the garbage bin, which was at the corner of the room and said, "we don't have much time, we have to find that old man before anything else happens."

George was still quiet and he was looking at her as she was trying to control herself and concentrate, started thinking deeply and again tried to look like a detective, and said. "The dark hole between the stars! It means that old man in black had entered a dark hole between the stars! What does that mean? Where exactly is that dark hole, anyway?"

They were thinking for a few second, that suddenly something sparked in Elena's mind and said. "that hole must be a black hole in space."

George, "what the heck are the space black holes?" Elena walked toward the bookcase and pulled out a very thick book which made the other books fall on each other toward the left side of the book case like domino.

She raised her eye brows and shrugged her shoulders and said. "Oops......, I'll put them in order later."

As she was holding the book in her hands and turning the pages walked toward George. The cover had picture of sky full of stars that the brighter ones were more noticeable and they were connected to each other by dotted line, which looked like a bear when you looked at it. She turned the pages until she got to page 417 and then as she was moving her finger in a zigzag on the page, she stopped on paragraph three and said, "here", black holes. Read this here to understand what I mean,"

George took the book very slowly in his hands and read these sentences very carefully: "different stars with different masses might change to white dwarf or neutron star. But still something else might happen to these dying stars. If the leftover of mass of the core after the explosion of Nova cloud or super Nova or even hyper Nova is three times more than sun's mass .In this situation gravitatonal collapse happens and it will continue to a point that even the fundamental structure of the object cannot bear it. This star will collapse inside itself so much that its mass becomes zero. In this situation the density of that spot in space-time will be endless. Of course whenever somewhere in space time there is enough material, and it is suddenly concentrated again, a black hole is made. Schwarzschild found this subject that if the radius of a mass gets small enough, the space-time around it will be extremely bended. And we can assume this object has high gravity or even infinity. In this situation nothing is able to escape from it, even light! As we can see in Schwarzschild radius something strange happens. It seems the clocks work endlessly and if a message in specific minute like 'T' is sent, it won't get to a further radius, unless the time is passed endlessly. In fact, signals with less radius of Schwarzschild radius will never been sent and never come out. Therefore an object with full mass that is in Schwarzschild radius won't have any light in the world and it will be invisible. This object is black hole or space black hole. Inside something like this is so far away from us that you think it's another world. This world could be so different it could violate Albert Einstein's laws."

George closed the book and as he was putting it on the desk said." It's very interesting! A space black hole!

Elena, "but where is this black hole?"

George took a deep breath through his mouth and right away blew it out of his closed lips showing her, he was tired and nothing comes to his mind.

He side, "we'd better take a break and rest our minds. What do you think?!"

The same time there were two knocks on the door and peter's voice was heard, saying. "Lunch is ready. Madam."

Elena sighed and said, "It seems, we have no choice, Ok, agree." "after lunch we'll think about It." and then raised her voice and told Peter, "we've coming."

George, with a sharp, silver color knife was cutting his steak when the movement of knife stopped on his steak. For a minute he stopped eating. It seemed a point has attracted his attention. he stared at Elena who was sitting on the other side of the table and side," what that strange symbol means?" it was in Mr. Faulkner's safe and in Nostradamus' hand writings."

She was still chewing that said, "I agree with you" "maybe he used this symbol as a code. A code that in an unknown way is connected to recent events"

He put a piece of steak in his mouth with a fork, chewed it a bit, then looked at the paintings on the ceiling and said, "We'lldiscover this code."

A few minutes later, they entered Elena's office. She put her palms on the desk, pressed them and jumped on it, sat and said, "Our knowledge is like small spots that by finding the relation between them and connecting them to each other we can find the answer. Of course, we should know which point should be connected to which point.

Well ,we better start our work with Nostradamus prophecies."

Before, she had come down from the desk, George pointed to the book which she was sitting next to, on the desk and said, "exactly like the picture on the cover of that book, you can only understand a bear is hidden between all those stars, when you connect the brighter stars to each other. Did I give a good example?"

Elena listening to these words, stared at the picture on the cover and after a few second in a rush jumped down from the desk and dashed toward her laptop and one more time looked at the pictures Arthur had sent her and suddenly her face expression changed and shouted excitedly, "George! You're a genius. You discovered the Nostradamus code."

George. "I really don't understand what you're saying."

Elena, "just a second, you'll know in a minute." she connected her laptop to a small printer and printed the two pictures, then took a yellow marker out of a drawer in her desk and connected the stars that were brighter in the printed pictures with a line, then with the same naughtiness said, "now, what do you see?" In amazement, the same symbol appeared in front of George's stunned eyes.

He said, "this is wonderful. It's exactly the same symbol."

Again she sat behind her laptop and said, "now we have to see if any black holes in the area of the pictures are discovered or not?" she typed the word NASA and pressed Enter. After half an hour research, she succeeded to find an answer, the answer was positive. She was right. In the direction of those pictures a little further, NASA had discovered a black hole and this was the beginning of their adventure.

13-Stealing Discovery Shuttle

Her golden hair was dancing to the breeze and their legs were hanging about seven meters above the ground as they were sitting side by side on the stone of the window ledge which was hardly half a meter watching the sunset.

Elena was swinging her legs that said, "I'm going to the space black-hole. I have to take revenge on behalf of Mrs. Hopkins and find the rest of missing prophecies. Maybe the rest of them can help me prevent the terrible events which are going to happen in future and destroy earth, otherwise all people may die. But what do you want to do George?, "from now on we have difficult and dangerous task ahead of us. Are you coming with me, or do you prefer to stay here?"

He stared into her eyes with passion in his eyes. It was a romantic moment. He told her with feelings deep through his heart. "I'll never leave you alone, no matter how dangerous this is. I don't care. If I have to die, I want to die beside you. I'll come with you, but I still don't know how you want to travel to space black hole." she looked at him kindly, smiled and said, "I have to continue what my father started."

George, "what do you mean?"

She took his hand in hers and said, "come with me! I have to show you something."

They turned toward Elena's office on the ledge of the window, put their hands on the window frame and jumped on the floor of the room very slowly. As she was holding his hand, walked toward the room which was in front of her office on the left of stairs, with her right hand she turned the shiny, steel knob and opened the door. It was a dark room and their shadows were on the wooden floor in the bright rectangle, but part of light from the chandeliers which were hanging from the ceiling in the hall made their shadows stretch so much that their heads were on the wall in the room in front of them. She turned on the light and a very beautiful and exquisite room appeared. The floor, book shelves, a few sofas and chairs, even the picture frame that held a picture of a middle aged man in space suit were all made of pine.

George, "you wanted to show me your father's room?!!" without answering him, she walked straight toward the bookshelves that covered the left wall from floor to ceiling. She pushed a few books on the side, and pressed the small golden button which was hidden behind the books. They vibrated slightly and one part of the shelves moved to the left and another one to the right, and a secret way appeared in the middle. She pointed to George and said, "Hurry! Come with me! There are still two more light switches left to the real surprise."

They both walked in the dark path, after a few steps she switched on another light. Now, George was able to see the elevator which was a few steps away from them.

They got in and it started going down. It seemed they were going toward the center of the earth; George was preparing himself for the big surprise Elena had promised. The elevator went down about sixty meters and then very slowly stopped.

Elena, "well, we're here"

The sound of their steps as they walked on the hard ground under their feet could be heard, until they found themselves in front of a big, steel door. There were some buttons beside the door. Elena pressed some numbers as the code for the door and after seconds the huge door started to move. They walked into dense darkness. He didn't know where they were, Until Elena put her finger on a light switch, she had promised and turned it on. 120 powerful projectors that were installed in the ceiling, sixty meters above lit up a very big area which was more like an underground hall.

On the wall, at the end of the hall there was a very big hole that the end wasn't clear, like a very, very big mole had dug it, a mole with a body of 25 meters in diameter. About one hundred meter from George, There was a monstrous cylindrical shape machine, which had the same diameter as the hole in the wall, and a number of big steel doors were on the concrete walls of the hall. But George was looking at something else. He had bent his neck and head back and he was staring up, but not the ceiling. To a very big orange a fuel tank which was about 50 meters in height. There were two white fuel tanks in the shape of rockets on the sides of the orange fuel tank.

As George was staring at them said, "OH …my God!! What's that?!!"

Elena, "when my father noticed he had cancer about a year ago, he didn't want to die in his bed! He was an adventurous person. Since, he saw, he was dying soon, he wanted to experience his biggest life adventure, and he wanted to do something that no one had ever had the ability or the courage to do. He decided to go to a space black- hole. He decided to do this with his long term friend discovery shuttle. He had lots of memory with this shuttle and he didn't want his dear shuttle die in museum and he in bed. He wanted to die in his favorite shuttle while he was experiencing his biggest adventure in history.

Therefore he talked to a group of his trustworthy friends in space organization about it. Some of them were willing to make his last wish before death come through. Of course my father had to pay for this project. Himself and he decided to spent more money and use other countries experts in this project. With the use of T.B.M and spending lots of money and time this underground base was made by them. They provided old the facilities to start the shuttle flight control center. After they finished building the liquid fuel tank and two rockets for solid fuel, it was time to steal the discovery shuttle from the space museum in Washington, which was the hardest part of the plan.

If they succeeded in stealing the shuttle, they had to add the essential parts which had been taken away before taking the shuttle to the museum. Some changes had to be made in the shuttle then it was ready to fly. My father's plan to steal the shuttle was to use this T.B.M (Tunnel Boring Machine) which was used to make this place. They were going to make a tunnel under the **Smithsonian** National Air and Space Museum in Washington DC.

Steal the shuttle at night and bring it here. They started the tunnel, but before they could reach the museum, my father died of cancer. Everything was left unfinished and this place has been forgotten. But now, I think, it is time for me to follow my father's footsteps and finish what he had started."

George. "Then being adventurous is in your blood, you took it after your father!! He must have been a really unique person?!"

Elena, "yes, he was a unique person". She stopped for a moment and then continued, "by the way, Do you want me to show you different parts of this place?!"

George, "of course, sure".

First they walked toward the Monstrous cylindrical machine, she hit it slowly a few times and with the same naughtiness she always talks said, "this little mouse made that hole in the wall". "This is the T.B.M, I talked to you about. In fact, this is the biggest drill in the world".

George looked the machine and said, "The biggest drill in the world Ha!! A really suitable title."

In fact, it was the biggest T.B.M made in the world. A few minutes later, Elena showed him a very big steel door which the word "Exit" was written on it in red.

Behind this door was a private road with the slope of 26^0 which went to the surface and when it came out from the center of the earth led to a wider road. She explained to him that all the facilities were taken down through this road. She took his hand in hers and walked toward another steel door. The door opened and the white lights that were installed in the ceiling lit up the room. It was a big hall with ceiling which was 4 meters high. There were three huge monitors on the black wall at the end of the room, there were nineteen curved rows with computerized systems and in each row there were 3 or 4 monitors the same size as personal computer. The rows had the same distance from each other and they were toward the black wall which was the back of the room. In fact, they were set the way that tens of people who were going to work in this room could see those three huge monitors completely.

George, "where is this?"

Elena, "well, this is space shuttle flight control room".

George, "how your father wanted to get all these experts for controlling space shuttle flight?"

Elena, "with a 300 million dollar payment all problems can be solved, and you can bring experts from all over the world here. This is exactly what I am going to do in the next few days, Not only the American experts but also some experts who are working in Russia and china.

Well, we don't have anything else to do here; Now, I want to show you another room where we have lots of things to do tomorrow."

Another steel door opened, lots of yellow lights lit the room.

The equipment in the room attracted George's attention. A room made of glass, Small enough for one person, a glass spherical object made of bullet proof glass which had places for wrists and feet, and was inside a cube shape machine and it had the ability to turn around itself in different directions.

The speed and the directions this machine was turning, was controlled by computer system. There was a special engine which was in the ground in vertical position, that its blades were toward the ceiling and there was steel net over it, and ..., but except the equipment in the room, there was a very small, but very deep pool at the corner of the hall.

It was about 30 meters deep. As George was looking around himself in confusion, Elena started to introduce the equipment, and she started with the glass room, "this is the vacuum chamber; with this you can increase your body strength in situations when the air pressure is very low. It can decrease the air inside so much that the air. Pressure reaches zero; of course, any human in this situation will die for sure". Then she walked toward that spherical object which was inside the cube machine. Elena with the keyboard which was on the machine made the necessary adjustments and then pressed the green button, and the spherical object started to turn around itself. Elena said, "this machine can improve your strength toward spinning and turning that might happen in situations when you are weightless."

Then she went toward that engine in the ground, with the steel net over it on the ground. When the engine Started a very strong currant toward up and ceiling started to blow.

The current due to the blades turning was so strong that if a person would stand on the steel net, his weight would be neutralized, and it would cause him to be suspended in the air.

Elena put on a bat shape cloth and jumped on the steel net, as she was suspending in the air said, "This special engine helps you to experience the weightlessness, the same thing that happens to you in the space shuttle. Now, please turn it off."

Her feet touched the ground again. George looked at the corner of the room and said, "Good thing, you have a pool here, whenever you feel tired, you can play in the water!!"

Elena, "a pool which is 30 meters deep is not a good place to play with water".

George, "you mean this pool is 30 meters deep?!!"

They walked toward the pool; she dropped a heavy weight which was connected to a long rope with numbers on it. Into the pool and told George, "read the number on the rope."

George, "exactly 30 meters, but why this pool was made so deep?!"

Elena, "being in deep water is a kind of exercise for our body to tolerate more pressure. Well, except these exercises you have to learn flying a shuttle tomorrow" "Flying I can teach you myself."

George, "training as a pilot why?!"

Elena, "A space shuttle needs at least two pilots, so you have to learn how to fly."

George thought to himself for a second and then said,

"Well.... How about charley for this job?! At least he knows how to fly a helicopter. I'm sure he can learn how to fly a shuttle faster than me."

Elena, "How, do you expect me to ask charley to come with us to a space black hole?" "Going to a space block hole is a trip to a complete unknown place. It's matter of life and death. He has no reason to risk his life and come with us."

George thought again and this time said, "What do you think of Thomas? We'd better talk to him about this, to find his mother's murderer, he will help us for sure, and he can learn flying a shuttle faster than me and He can join us in this trip".

Elena glared at him and said, "Thomas?! Are you joking?!! He would never believe our words. He always believed whatever his mother said about Nostradamus were superstitions. If I tell him about this no lonely he doesn't help us but he will also try to stop us and would wreck everything. George you are the only one who can do this."

George, "but it's a very difficult task and our time is limited". She held his left arm in her hand, stared into his eyes and warmly said, "You can do this. I have faith in you".

George, "I hope, I can do it".

Elena, "I'm sure you are up to it".

Again the beep on the phone was making noise until Elena said, "hello, Mr. Huffman, this is Elena…"

There were lots of phone calls like this. She was sitting in her office, making phone calls to about 15 people before going to underground base and starting training George for astronaut. In fact, she was preparing everything for her project, stealing the space shuttle and going to the space black hole.

Because of this, she called her father's old friends and her friends who she used to work with in the space organization. Ten out of sixteen phone calls were successful and they were willing to work with her. She took a deep breath and got ready to go to the underground base.

George with very loud voice as he was pushing his eyes closed said, "stop it".

Elena pressed the red button on the keyboard and the glass spherical object stopped spinning. George stagger out of the glass room, sat on the ground, put his head in a plastic bin and throw up whatever he had eaten. Elena came close to him as she was holding a white tissue and said, "You have only 15 minutes to rest, then your pilot training class starts."

He cleaned his mouth with the tissue and got up.

A very loud sound rumbled in the air and the monstrous machine's drills started to turn and dig. This machine except the spinning movement was going forward with the pressure of jacks, and the result of these two movements was digging the dirt inside the tunnel. The dirt was then came out through the control doors which were in the head of drills and sent to a 50 meter conveyor belt along the side of the machine and after a long process finally it was taken out of the underground base by trucks. Elena was standing next to George and as they were observing the process, she was explaining about the machine. An engineer who was wearing a hard yellow hat said loudly, "turn off the machine!, we'll start again, in two hours."

Finally the rumbling sound stopped. George and Elena were inside the tunnel beside that long convey or belt. George pointed to one of hundreds of thick pipes that were coming out of the wall inside the tunnel and with curiosity asked, "what are these pipes for?"

Elena, "they have the most important role in this project; each pipe is connected to a big source of concrete. Each source holds about forty thousand cubic meters concrete. After we succeed in stealing the space shuttle and brought it here through this tunnel, then these pipes start their work. They will pump hundred thousand cubic meters of concrete into the tunnel very fast and seal the tunnel, so nobody can follow us."

Then she looked at her watch and said, "well, your break is over, what I want to teach you today is very important. You have to concentrate very hard". "We'd better run."

Weakness and pale color started to appear in George's face which the skin was swollen. He couldn't stand it anymore. Elena pushed the button very fast and when the small glass room's door opened, very fast she took off the special hat which was for breathing oxygen, from George's head and pulled him out of the vacuum chamber. It took minutes until he was normal again.

Elena, "compare to last month you have progressed well and you endured the condition inside the room very well".

Then without waiting to hear any comment from George, took a black marker and got ready to start her lesson on the white board. They had to take advantage of the time they had. Every minute was valuable.

It was a quiet night and the **Smithsonian** museum was glowing under the moon light. The Discovery Shuttle was soundly asleep inside the museum that the sharp and powerful drills of Tunnel Boring Machine made a hole on the floor of the museum and the rumbling sound echoed in the room for seconds. After a few minutes Elena and George got close to the shuttle with flash lights in their hands. The circumference light of George flash light was beaming one of the shuttle's wings and the word '**Discovery**' appeared. They examined the shuttle very carefully to find the right place for the chrome cables.

After they attacked three chrome cables to the shuttle Very carefully, Elena with her finger pointed to the driver who was sitting in a big bulldozer to move. They pulled the T.B.M out of the tunnel very fast and now a huge bulldozer was pulling the discovery shuttle behind itself in the tunnel. When the shuttle was moved to the underground base. hundreds of thick pipes that were coming out of tunnel's wall pumped the concrete into the tunnel with really high pressure and fast. After hours there was no sign of the tunnel and concrete was taking its place. Now, the project of stealing the discovery shuttle had ended success fully.

14- Trip to the Space Black Hole

A naked hand went through the steamed mirror in the shower and George's face appeared. He was staring at the burned mark and its pattern on his left arm. He was going to touch it, that suddenly Elena's voice behind the bath room door said, "George! We don't have much time to our flight. Hurry up!"

It's been two months since they stole the shuttle. Now George was a shuttle pilot after going through necessary training and hard exercises. During this time the shuttle experts were able to provide the engines and other parts which had been taken away, when they had moved the shuttle to the museum, and they had installed them. It had cost Elena 400 million dollars. George took his towel and dried his body.

Elena glanced at her Katana swords, held them in her hand with her Backpack, and walked toward the hidden door at her father's room to get on the shuttle. There was a lot of noise inside the space shuttle flight control room. There were experts from different countries sitting behind the computer systems.

Pictures appeared on the three huge monitors, liquid fuel tank and solid fuel tanks were filled. Elena with pride and honor stared at the space shuttle which was on the launch plat form in the middle of underground base and drops of tears came down from the corner of her eyes maybe she wished her father were alive and could join her on this trip. At the moment she was making his dream come through. She was still staring at the shuttle that suddenly she felt the weight of a hand on her shoulder.

George. "I'm ready. Don't you want to get on the shuttle?" As she was trying to hide the tears on her face said, "OH, you're right, it's time to go."

After they were on board, the space shuttle, the big automatic doors which were installed about 60 meters up in the ceiling started to open slowly. The launch platform with the shuttle on it, started to go up by huge hydraulic jacks. After a distance of 60 meters, when it was on the ground level stopped.

Now the launch platform with the space shuttle both were in the middle of Elena's green yard. Peter was standing in one of the balconies of the building, cleaning his tears with a white tissue. Life had no meaning for him without Madam, but he couldn't discourage madam from going on this trip. It was too late, because the countdown to launch had started, 10, 9, 8, 7, 6, 5, 4, 3, 2, and 1. Very thick white smoke came out of the end of the space shuttle and it started flying in the sky. Minutes were passing so fast, Elena and George were sitting on their special seats.

The shuttle had gone a long distance and was really far from the earth. George was thinking to himself. He knew perfectly in a few minutes they will enter a space black hole and it will suck them in. It wasn't clear what will happen to them when they entered the black hole and what events are waiting for them. Maybe they both die and maybe this is the last time he sees her. His heart was beating so fast. He wanted to tell her, how he felt about her before anything happens. In the past few months they both had been so busy that George didn't have the chance to tell her about his feelings heart. These last few minutes were the last chance he had and he didn't want to waste them. Although his heart was pounding fast and his breathing had gotten fast, he took two deep breaths. Elena, noticed the change in George, she looked at him. His familiar and shinny eyes, like the reflection of two end candle lights at the bottom of a well were glowing in front of her.

Elena's condition was changing now. It was obvious; she could see his passion and love by looking at his eyes. The same love and passion were in her eyes. Therefore, before George could say anything went forward as she was looking at his eyes, she put her lips, close to his. He could feel the heat in her face unwillingly he pat his face close to hers. As he was only a few centimeters to kiss her lips, suddenly the alarm went off and announced they were getting close to a space black hole. A sensor was put in the shuttle that could measure the intensity of magnetic field and could calculate how close they were to a space black hole, they were very close now. She was startled and said,

"OH my God, we are close to a black hole and I haven't taken that." George who was completely confused said, "what are you talking about?!!"

Elena said anxiously, "you just sit here, I'll be back."

Then she opened her seatbelt and got up, as she was in the air suspended, moved toward an opening which led to another part of the shuttle. George listened to her and didn't leave his seat even though he was very nervous.

Time was passing fast. It's been 3 minutes since Elena left. There was no sign of her. He couldn't wait any more and was really worried, and nervous. He got up and moved through the same opening. After passing he couldn't believe his eyes. It was a terrifying scene. Elena's body was in the air with one of her swords into her heart up to the handle. Her eyes were open, staring at the ceiling of the shuttle and her clothes full of blood. Suddenly an absolute darkness covered everywhere and George felt an awful pressure on his body. He had entered a space black hole now.